The Mood Ring

Diaries

The Mood Ring Diaries

Poetry by

Jessica D. Thompson

© 2025 Jessica D. Thompson. All rights reserved.
This material may not be reproduced in any form, published,
reprinted, recorded, performed, broadcast,
rewritten or redistributed without
the explicit permission of Jessica D. Thompson.
All such actions are strictly prohibited by law.

Cover design by Shay Culligan
Cover image by Evgeni Tcherkasski

ISBN: 978-1-63980-692-8

Kelsay Books
502 South 1040 East, A-119
American Fork, Utah 84003
Kelsaybooks.com

For all sky daughters

Acknowledgments

The author wishes to thank the following journals which first gave her poems a home, sometimes in earlier forms:

Appalachian Review: "Chasing Beauty," "Diana"

Bloodroot: "Spent"

Circe's Lament: Anthology of Wild Women Poetry (Accents Publishing): "Diana"

Daybreak and Deep (Kelsay Books, 2022): "Still Life," "The Mood Ring Diaries"

Gyroscope Review: "At Seventeen," "Reading Plath at Goodyear"

Kansas City Voices (Whispering Prairie Press): "The Grandmother Who Fell from the Sky"

The Lunar Codex Project (comprised of three cosmic time capsules of art, music, and poetry that was part of the payload of SpaceX Astrobotic Technologies' Griffin Lander, which landed on the moon in 2024): "The Grandmother Who Fell from the Sky"

Nerve Cowboy: "My Newest Almost Boyfriend," "Still Life," "The Night I Got My Period"

ONE ART, a journal of poetry: "Our 3-Ring Kitchen"

Sheila-Na-Gig: "Chimera," "Sleep Walking"

Still: The Journal: "The Mood Ring Diaries"

Thimble: "Dolphin"

Tipton Poetry Journal: "Hollow Bones"

Women Speak, Women of Appalachia Project (Sheila-Na-Gig Editions): "Cradlesong for a Future Crone," "Sky Daughters"

With gratitude to these kind and talented poets—the best workshop teachers any aspiring writer could hope for: Jesse Graves, Rebecca Gayle Howell, Simone Muench, Linda Parsons, and Marianne Worthington.

I am indebted to members of my writer's group, Linda Neal Reising and Mark Williams, and give thanks for their many years of friendship and good counsel.

With great appreciation and love to Mary O'Dell, President and Founder of the Green River Writers, who, long ago, took me under her wing.

And finally, to all my sisters, to the women I have met in conferences, in classrooms, in emergency rooms and shelters, and to those who marched (and continue to march) in the streets, I stand with you. May our voices never be silenced.

Contents

Diary Entry dated August 2, 1962

The Mood Ring Diaries	17
Hollow Bones	19
Our 3-Ring Kitchen	20
The Night I Got My Period	22

Diary Entry dated March 11, 1969

At Seventeen	27
The Grandmother Who Fell from the Sky	29
Sleep Walking	32
Cradlesong for a Future Crone	35

Diary Entry dated May 18, 1985

Diana	39
Chimera	40
Chasing Beauty	42
Dolphin	43

Diary Entry dated April 17, 1990

Spent	47
My Newest Almost Boyfriend	48
Reading Plath at Goodyear	50
Still Life	51

Diary Entry dated June 23, 2024

Sky Daughters

Foreword

There is a prophetic quality in the way the poems of *The Mood Ring Diaries* summon reverie from life's rituals and rites-of-passage.

Jessica Thompson's poems are eloquently honest, engaging the reader with a quiet but profound sense of wonder at the landmark moments in our lives.

Each work is a portal to self-discovery through the stages of life, both solemn and ebullient:

> *When my girlish body changed, I became a dress maker's / mannequin, my mouth shut. My heart a stone hut.*
>
> *The bubbling laughter, / our lullaby voices. / The bluish whites of our eyes, / our long, unencumbered hair.*

The familiar is presented under the lens of desire, longing, and the recitation of simple tasks in which we arrange our lives.

Thompson's skill as a writer is like a sleight-of-hand, her poetry a subtle yet profoundly rendered vehicle for personal metamorphosis.

The alchemy of her language is that it renders the familiar as mythic, the small moments from youth as sensually epic: *Invisible, we unfurled our laughter out into a darkening sky. / This is the oldest language—our tongues tasting / of honeysuckle and heat lightning.*

—Mindy Kronenberg, Poet, Professor at SUNY Empire State University, Editor of *Oberon* poetry magazine, and author of *Dismantling the Playground* and *Open*

I had to walk through the solar systems

before I found the first thread of my red dress.

—Edith Sodergran

(Translated by Stina Katchadourian)

August 2, 1962

Dear Diary,

In the beginning, we are little things,

copper tongued and shaken—

our breasts and knees rising,

hands cupped to mouths.

—Sarah

The Mood Ring Diaries

We lived in a time of iron lungs and Marlboro
men, where feral dogs with matted eyes

and rock-hard balls
ruled the streets of our childhood,

and rats multiplied in alleys
behind matchbox houses, and friends

spent a year in bed with rheumatic fever,
and the dust of summer stayed all year—

it lifted like prayers
from the footfalls of barefoot children,

and some of us would die young
from eating flecks of lead-based paint

picked like flower petals from plastered
walls. It tasted like cabbage roses

in faded wallpaper. It tasted like communion
wafers, and we were taught to sit up straight,

to smile—to be seen, but never heard.
Years later, we wore mood rings

to regulate our feelings,
and while our brothers went off to war,

we ran to altars
where bridesmaids stood like saints

in dotted Swiss dresses.
We wore the white of the sacrificed,

tied the knot, spent the rest of our lives
keeping everything inside

prized, knotty pine cabinets.

Hollow Bones

When we were children, we ran
in packs like young wolves,

crossing weed seeded fields
and dirt paths

into vacant wooded lots
between white framed houses.

We ran until we lost our breath,
until the pain in our sides stopped us.

Invisible arrows piercing
bird-like ribs. Our bones were hollow.

How else could we climb trees
with ease, or dare to jump

from tar papered roof tops.
Our grass-stained feet

lifted from the ground
by paper kites with trailing tails

born of rags.
Invincible, we unfurled

our laughter out into a darkening sky.
This is the oldest language—

our tongues tasting
of honeysuckle and heat lightning.

Our 3-Ring Kitchen

mother did the laundry
in our eat-in kitchen

like a trained circus animal
the wringer-washer

sat in a corner
waiting to be led

to the arena
linoleum floor patchwork

of green and white squares
marked with trails

from years of migrations
to a porcelain sink

the rubber hose
a curious trunk

this was the room
where my sister would sit

alone long after
the dishes were done

like a feral girl
refusing to eat

everything on her plate
her bible-black eyes

a flashing stampede
toward the ring leader

who ruled
from the head of our table

The Night I Got My Period

the New Albany Bulldogs played the Jeffersonville
Red Devils in the first football game of the season.

Leaning against my brother's '68 Chevelle,
parked next to the ticket booth,

bare legs under a mini skirt, soles
of my oxblood Bass Weejuns pushing

against the curb, just inches away from the gutter,
all my boy-crazy girlfriends leaving me behind.

I sold programs—
slick covers, deep folds down the middle,

all of them, one on top of the other,
next to my breast, my breath

visible with every sigh.
He sat on the visitors' side, smelled like English

Leather, his hair covering his collar—
so dark, so electric, so new.

When he leaned in, he put one hand on the Chevy,
the other reaching to take something from me,

and in a voice like no other, whispered
Where have you been? And it happened

right then, came without warning—
so dark, so electric, so new.

And I thought of the bullfrogs in Oliver's pond,
all those throats bubbling up, that sudden wet

urge driving our lives.

March 11, 1969

Dear Diary,

I miss the laughter of my sisters,

the sigh of fence posts, halos

of dried moths in an open field.

My skin smells of dirt and heat.

Take these from me—

snagged silk and crinoline.

—Annie

At Seventeen

I will wade out until my thighs are steeped in burning flowers.
                                                —e. e. cummings

A child, I fell in love with my own voice, performed one-act plays
in the backyard—a neighborhood boy for a stage hand. I wanted

to touch his perfect buzz cut with my fingertips. But, I did not.
It was summer. In the valley below, dragonflies mated in thin air.

The wildflowers were too beautiful to be picked—goblets
of scarlet clover, fire pinks, maiden-hair ferns, the dog-toothed

violet. Always running free—boys with trunks made of rough
bark. I was not allowed. I was not allowed to climb trees.

Still, I thought, my knees have bled before, yes—
I have lifted the asperous scabs, watched as new skin grew back.

The beginning of scars. With alabaster bodies, boys
lived in forts, carried shields, and drew boundaries. I lived inside

books. When my girlish body changed, I became a dress maker's
mannequin, my mouth shut. My heart a stone hut.

All too rapidly, the second-hand of mother's wound-too-tight
watch, all her fears—transformed into a wedding dress.

Like a ballet of swans, young girls hovered nearby, swooning
over freshly dyed baby-blue pumps. Then came the many buttons,

a veil I fought to see through, flowers I threw, rice in the air—
given away, at seventeen, by my father. White horses

turned back into mice. I bled the first time it happened
while lying on a slice of honeymoon bed.

Proof that I was good.
In time, I learned to focus on grandmother's lace handkerchief

draped over a lamp shade. *Grandmother, why?*
I have heard it said that tears can split wood. Let us gather kindling

into the folds of our dresses. Let us carry it inside stone huts.
We can build a fire that will never go out.

We will feed it wildflowers.
Sweep away the ash

from our crinolines, our paper dolls, the petals of ox-eye daisies—
I love him. I love him not.

The Grandmother Who Fell from the Sky

My grandmother fell from the sky
when she was six years old.

The mayflies arrived at the same time,
rising in a bright cloud over the pond.

I have the black and white photo
to prove it. She wore a summer dress

that day, thin anklets, and shoes
sturdy enough for the journey—

a haze of mayflies forming a crown
above her crow-black hair.

She arrived carrying a kitten.
I have often wondered

if the kitten was falling from the sky,
too, and she caught him

in her sun-gold arms while in dreamtime.
My grandmother had a crooked smile.

I have always thought this was the result
of her entering earth's atmosphere.

You know the kind of smile I mean—
the one where one side is higher

than the other end, as if gravity
had no power in that sacred opening.

She had her own language.
There were times when we were together

and she would slip into another dimension.
Mostly times when we walked

among her flowers—her garden an asterism
of pentas, star jasmine, ferns, and moss

roses that grew in the cracks of her sidewalk.
She spoke to the flowers as she would speak

to anyone—gently. And I swear,
they would respond—their heads nodding

in the wind. Once, during a new moon,
while we lay on our backs watching the sky

turn blue-black, she pointed to the first star
and whispered, *I'll be going back there.*

When she died at the young age
of seventy-three, I dreamed of her ascension

back into the sky. I watched as the heavens
reclaimed her body—her streaming hair,

high cheek bones, tiny waist, and racehorse
ankles. I witnessed her smile

straightening, made new—as she flew
higher and higher, and higher still.

Sleep Walking

when my sister was a   little girl

she would glide

through the rooms

of our house

       sleep   walking

her round face

luminescent   innocent

her marble feet

tiny toes

sprouting beneath

       the

             ruffle of a night

gown

             stowaway

on a wooden ship

and we

my other sisters and I

                        a pod of

                                  dolphins

riding the waves

                                    alongside her

it was later

and too   soon

after she had grown

into an amazing woman

that a monster of the   deep

came   changed

the makeup of her blood

again

we rode the   waves

that tossed her   followed

her   to a shore of singing

                           light

from which we had to

turn and leave her

Cradlesong for a Future Crone

Standing at the sink, wrist deep
in water, my hands the heart

of this shiplapped room—
remembering my sisters

in the kitchen of our youth.
Doing the dishes.

The bubbling laughter,
our lullaby voices.

The bluish whites of our eyes,
our long, unencumbered hair.

A step stool at the sink,
the heavy pots,

the sweeping of the floor.
Shipwrecked

when one of us left—
the slamming of a screen door.

This salty water.

May 18, 1985

Dear Diary,

I sit in the dark—holding up the sky.

Mother, mater, most maternal.

—D. M.

Diana

In her dreams, she sees rabbits
running in the woods.

White ones swallow black
ones, head first and whole.

She labors to push them out
before they stop

breathing. In her mind,
she has infinite children

with cherub faces.
They bring her what they kill.

She eats the hearts first,
before they go bad—

as all hearts will.

Chimera

Entering the bloodstream through the placenta,
fetal cells embed themselves

into the mother's skin, brain, heart—
where they can stay for decades,

a phenomenon known as microchimerism,
from the Greek word *chimera*—

a mythical creature made from the parts
of different animals. There once was a boy

who found bones on his grandfather's farm,
believed them to be from a dinosaur.

At times, I can convince myself that boy
is thriving, living in another galaxy.

Once upon a time, I sewed stars
onto a Little League cap—one for each home

run, scrubbed stains from a snow-white
uniform.

I taught you to dance. Remember
the blue pinstripe shirt and the red suspenders?

It was 1984. I took you and one of your friends
to your first concert—Lover Boy.

But sometimes mothers become myths
and little boys grow into minotaurs—

their rogue cells orbiting the souls
of women who spin aimlessly inside black holes.

Chasing Beauty

She takes up too much space
with her books, her soup

bowls. Breaks a bone
rather than cope

with brokenness.
There are so many ways

to do it—
pistol, razor blade, river.

But she cannot accept
the ugliness, the spectacle,

when all her life
she has chased after beauty.

So she starts keeping bees,
growing plots of oleander

because she read somewhere
that their flowers

will poison you
if you eat the honey

made by bees
that have savored the nectar.

Dolphin

At low tide on a barren beach,
a sun-bleached dolphin skull.

Nothing left but bone.
Strewn nearby,

weathered vertebrae—
medallions,

each shaped
like a uterus with ovaries.

I slide one onto the silver
chain around my neck—

a crucifix for an old woman
with a forgiving heart.

Relentless, the breakers roll
about like a die cupped

in the defiant fist of an aged
mariner. The dolphin's

one-hundred teeth
scattered in the deep

like a broken strand of pearls.

April 17, 1990

Dear Diary,

Certain things grow best in the dark—

like the root crops of parsnip, carrot, and beet.

I kneel before sedum, alyssum, bleeding hearts.

Deadhead petunias. Condemn spent blossoms

to bedrock. I tend to memories of old desires—

driving home down empty streets, turning a key

inside a worn lock.

—Beth

Spent

Last night, a beautiful man
ran past me in the dark.

Gliding by, he spoke,
How are you?

The inflection in his voice,
like water

spilling from a pail.
I remember our

breath. I remember the act
of becoming spent.

This morning,
I found one of your

cigarettes in the garage,
the tip of which

had been clasped
so passionately, your

teeth marks were still visible.

My Newest Almost Boyfriend

arrived with the appearance of Comet
Neowise which won't be visible

again for another 7,000 years.
That's a long time to wait for comets

or boyfriends. He seduced me
while traipsing through his run-down

Italianate. He seduced me with his
black Mercedes, his hanging plants,

his cat named GiGi. After three dates,
he crooned, *You just might be the one*;

and, *Sweetheart, you better start
writing our vows.*

I think he might be the devil.
I mean the way he gets me, sweeps

me off my feet. He can see the future.
Last night he whispered, *Design*

my library room, then pleaded,
Bring your dog, move into this sexy

house. Did I mention there is a Juliet
balcony? We know how that story ends.

He says he is nervous because I am
so articulate, so gorgeous.

He drinks too much.
He breaks my heart.

But not in ways you might imagine.
In the way he prunes his roses—

there on his hands and knees.
Above us, there is Neowise—

portent of disaster. The way the words
Have you had any work done?

roll off his tongue.

Reading Plath at Goodyear

The tulips are too excitable.
—Sylvia Plath

When a blonde god at the tire store
checks my pressure, I cannot help

but notice his lips—
how delicately they part

as he starts to speak—
like two petals of a perfect tulip—

as if they had been waiting
there all afternoon, in a tall

vase on a windowsill,
for a sudden rush

of summer wind to stir
just so, and all at once,

they found themselves within a spell,
broken only by the knelling of a bell.

Still Life

After a time, you stop looking
in mirrors, keep

the company of trees, refuse
cream in coffee,

linger
wide-eyed in darkness.

You stop reciting prayers.
Now I lay me.

Everything
has become a prayer—

sunlit window,
bath towel drying on a chair,

loose threads on the hem
of your red dress.

June 23, 2024

Dear Diary,

Sky Daughters

*We flee into a stand of trees
in search of scriptures*

*written upon leaves. Envying
the braided bark of hickories,*

*we storm rushing streams,
ghost horses with red manes.*

*Our moss-soft names
burn like fire-*

*pinks with petals
of polished flames.*

*With hearts billowing
like cumulus clouds—we are*

*the descendants
of rain.*

—Diane

Notes

Diary entries dated August 2, 1962, March 11, 1969, and May 18, 1985 are centos comprised of lines or phrases taken from poems by Hadara Bar-Nadav, Mary Biddinger, Kristy Bowen, Nickole Brown, Suzanne Buffam, Susan Kinsolving, and Mathias Svalina.

About the Author

Jessica D. Thompson's full-length poetry collection, *Daybreak and Deep* (Kelsay Books), was shortlisted for the 2024 Eugene and Marilyn Glick Indiana Authors Awards. *Daybreak and Deep* was also a finalist in the American Book Fest Best Books of 2022 for narrative poetry and was nominated for the Eric Hoffer Award. In addition, she co-authored the 2024 children's book, *When Animals Miss the Sun* (Brick Street Poetry).

Her poetry has appeared on *Verse Daily* and has been nominated for a Pushcart Prize. Her poems have been published in numerous journals and anthologies, among them: *Appalachian Review, Atlanta Review, Common Ground Review, Eclectica Magazine, Gyroscope Review, Lakeshore Review, ONE ART, a journal of poetry, Still: The Journal, The Midwest Quarterly, the Southern Review, Tipton Poetry Journal, Thimble, Tiferet Journal, Women Speak, Women of Appalachia Project* (Sheila-Na-Gig Editions), and *Next Indiana Campfires: a Trail Companion* (Indiana Humanities). Her awards include the James Baker Hall Memorial Prize in Poetry (New Southerner).

For many years, Jessica served as a crisis office volunteer, as well as a hospital and legal advocate for a battered women's shelter. She currently writes in a 1918 log cabin in the middle of a hardwood forest.

www.ingramcontent.com/pod-product-compliance
Lightning Source LLC
Chambersburg PA
CBHW031206160426
43193CB00008B/524